Social Media Marketing 2024

By

Jeff M. Blade

Table of Contents

Introduction

In the ever-evolving realm of the digital age, where information flows at the speed of light and connections span the globe in milliseconds, the significance of social media and digital marketing cannot be overstated. Our world has become intricately intertwined with the virtual, and in this dynamic landscape, businesses and individuals alike are compelled to harness the power of online platforms to thrive. As we embark on this exploration, "Digital Horizons: Navigating the Social Media Landscape for Success" seeks to be your guiding compass in the vast sea of possibilities that social media and digital marketing present. In the pages that follow, we will delve into the intricacies of analyzing online traffic, unlocking the secrets to monetizing social media, and understanding the paramount importance of online engagement.

The heartbeat of the digital era lies in the vast ocean of online traffic. Every click, every share, and every interaction leave a digital footprint that, when analyzed with precision, can unveil invaluable insights. In the first chapters of this book, we embark on a journey to decipher the language of analytics, demystifying the tools and techniques that empower you to comprehend the behavior of online visitors. From deciphering the intricacies of Google Analytics to understanding the impact of user demographics on your digital presence, we unravel the mysteries behind the numbers. We equip you with the knowledge to transform raw data into actionable strategies, ensuring that your online endeavors are not only seen but are also resonating with your target audience.

In a world driven by digital interactions, the ability to monetize social media platforms is a skill that can transform hobbies into careers and side hustles into thriving businesses. "Digital Horizons" provides you with a roadmap to navigate the landscape of social media monetization, whether you're a content creator, an entrepreneur, or a marketing professional. From sponsored content to affiliate marketing, we explore the myriad avenues available for turning your online presence into a revenue stream. Case studies and success stories from individuals and businesses who have mastered the art of turning clicks into currency serve as beacons of inspiration, guiding you on your journey to financial empowerment through digital channels.

Why does online traffic matter, and how does it shape the success of your digital endeavors? These are questions we address head-on, emphasizing the pivotal role that online engagement plays in the contemporary landscape. Beyond mere numbers, we delve into the qualitative aspects of online traffic – the conversations sparked, the communities formed, and the impact created. In an era where attention is a precious commodity, understanding the nuances of capturing and retaining your audience's interest becomes paramount. "Digital Horizons" aims to instill in you the significance of not just attracting online traffic but fostering meaningful connections that can withstand the ever-changing tides of the digital world. As the digital landscape expands, so does the competition for attention. To rise above the noise, it is imperative to have a robust strategy for increasing social media marketing traffic. This section of the book is dedicated to dissecting the tactics and techniques that can propel your online presence to new heights.

From mastering the algorithms of top social media platforms to crafting compelling content that resonates with your audience, we leave no stone unturned in our quest to equip you with the tools needed to stand out in the crowded digital arena. "Digital Horizons" serves as your guide to not only surviving but thriving in the ever-changing landscape of social media marketing. The digital horizon is dotted with a myriad of platforms, each offering unique opportunities and challenges. In the final chapters of this book, we take you on a tour of the top social media platforms, providing insights into the distinct features and strategies that can help you navigate each terrain.

Whether you're aiming to conquer the visual realm of Instagram, engage in real-time conversations on Twitter, or tap into the professional network of LinkedIn, "Digital Horizons" serves as your comprehensive guidebook. With expert advice and practical tips, we empower you to make informed decisions on where to invest your time and resources for maximum impact. As we embark on this journey together, "Digital Horizons" becomes more than a guidebook; it becomes a companion in your quest for digital success. Through the pages that follow, we invite you to explore, learn, and apply the principles that will unlock the full potential of your online presence. The digital horizon awaits – are you ready to set sail?

You will learn the following concepts from this book, to name a few examples:

- Digital Marketing vs Social Media Marketing
- What is social media management? Everything you need to know
- Top Social Media Sites to Consider for Your Brand in 2024
- How to Check Website Traffic
- How to use social listening to boost website traffic
- Online Tools to Increase Website Traffic
- Importance of Website Traffic in Your Business?

So, Let's Get Started:

Chapter No. 01

Digital Marketing vs Social Media Marketing

Businesses depend on digital and social media marketing tactics to promote their products, services, and other types of products and services. Both of them use the same social media platforms and tools in order to sell their products and services. It is common for the marketing professionals that carry out internet marketing campaigns to have backgrounds and areas of expertise that are complimentary to one another. The following distinctions will become apparent to you when you investigate the advantages and disadvantages of social media marketing and digital marketing.

1.1   What is Digital Marketing?
Learning about what digital marketing comprises is the first step toward gaining a grasp of the differences between social media marketing and digital marketing. Any method for promoting products or services online that relies on digital technology, such as the internet, is referred to as digital marketing. A variety of marketing strategies, such as pay-per-click advertising, video marketing, affiliate marketing, and social media marketing, are included in digital marketing.

1.2   What are Digital Marketing Tools?
When it comes to knowing the differences between social media marketing and digital marketing, digital marketing

tools are really necessary. It is necessary for contemporary digital marketers to be present on many forums in order to compete with other digital marketers. There are a number of digital marketing tools that may assist managers in reducing the amount of time they spend on information management and in improving the effectiveness of their marketing strategy. Listed below are some of the digital marketing tools that are available:

Marketing using social media that is organic

- Marketing via electronic mail
- Instruments for the production of content
- Paid marketing on social media platforms
- Social media platforms and apps
- Instruments for storing videos
- Analytical tools for websites
- SEO tools

1.3   What is Social Media Marketing?

One of the most significant differences between digital marketing and social media marketing is the fact that social media marketing is a subset of digital marketing and is carried out on various websites such as Instagram, Facebook, along with other similar platforms. The creation of content for a variety of social platforms and audiences, interaction with existing and prospective customers, and the establishment of an online presence are all components that are often included in social media marketing activities.

1.4   Building Blocks of Social Media Marketing

Comparatively speaking, social media marketing is an essential component of digital marketing as opposed to social media marketing. When it comes to marketing, social media marketing is a tool that is incredibly diverse and needs strong guiding principles. Within the realm of social media management, there are certain components that, when implemented, contribute to the development of an effective plan.

1.4.1 Strategy

A plan that has been well considered is essential to achieving success in social media. It is necessary for any social media platform to have guidelines that dictate what kinds of brand identities should be used, what kinds of content should be published, and what kinds of business goals should be pursued.

1.4.2 Consistency

When it comes to maintaining interaction on social media, consistency is very crucial. Make use of automated systems in order to keep releasing calendars on a monthly, weekly, or even daily basis.

1.4.3 Engagement

In order to monitor the success of a brand on social media, it is necessary to include social media management software solutions. The purpose of these technologies is to monitor and stay ahead of the mood and trends in the industry by tracking client responses and other information.

1.4.4 Data and Analytics

It is possible to find a large variety of analysis tools on social media networks. It is important to take the data seriously and make use of it in order to evaluate and quantify a variety of factors, including the efficacy of the efforts, brand awareness, and more.

1.4.5   Commercial Ads

It is possible that sponsored adverts on social media might be a highly rewarding investment if they are handled appropriately. Investing in high-quality campaigns that can be customized is the best way to ensure a satisfactory return on investment.

1.5   Digital Marketing vs. Social Media Marketing

Each and every digital marketing endeavor necessitates the implementation of social media techniques in order to guarantee long-term involvement and the effective use of marketing methods. In the event that you are considering digital marketing as opposed to social media marketing, it is important to keep in mind the following similarities and contrasts.

- Any marketing activity that is carried out on any and all digital platforms, both offline and online, is considered to be digital marketing. Although social media marketing is a kind of digital marketing that is conducted entirely online and makes use of social media websites, channels, and forums, it is not the same as Internet marketing.
- The goal of digital marketing is often to increase awareness by communicating with the target audience via a variety of touch points. On the other hand, social media marketing establishes a connection with the target audience by means of social platforms.
- In order to be successful, digital media must make investments in ads that are shown in prominent venues, such as billboards or television commercials. The success of social media, on the other hand, is

considerably dependent on the content strategy that is implemented.

- All modern forms of advertising that are based on electronic platforms are included in the overarching category of digital media. Because it makes use of social media interaction platforms, social media marketing is a distinctive sort of marketing.
- Sales are being predominantly increased by digital media. A wide range of commercial goals may be accomplished via the use of social media, including the study of competitors, the exposure of brands, and other purposes.

1.6   What Does a Typical Digital Marketing Campaign Include?

When comparing digital marketing to social media marketing, it is impossible to have a thorough conversation without also discussing digital marketing initiatives. Even though there are a great deal of diverse facets to digital marketing, the following are the components that are often included in a digital media marketing campaign.

- Use either paid search advertising or search engine optimization (SEO) and content strategy while engaging in search engine marketing.
- Promotions and campaigns on social media platforms, as well as the use of paid advertising on Facebook, Instagram, and other platforms, are included in the category of social media promotions.
- Promotions for the mobile market, including the development of applications and games and their published on the Apple Store and Google Play.

- Email marketing refers to the practice of promoting goods or services via the use of email marketing campaigns.

1.7 Why Should You Include Social Media Marketing in Your Digital Marketing Campaign?

In today's digital age, marketing via social media has evolved into an absolute must. It is necessary for every business that wants to increase their audience abroad and get their brand in front of clients if they want to achieve these goals.

When compared to other forms of digital media marketing, social media marketing initiatives have a tendency to create answers for the majority of firms in a more expedient manner. If companies and brands want to make the most of the advantages and return on investment that social media marketing offers, they need to include extra digital marketing aspects into their digital marketing plan in addition to social media marketing.

1.8 Which Is More Effective: Social Marketing or Digital Marketing?

When it comes to marketing, digital marketing and social media marketing both have the potential to make substantial contributions, depending on the goals of a firm. In comparison to social media, digital media has been around for quite some time. Social media is very new.

When it comes to marketing, social media marketing has swiftly become one of the most important means of marketing for many different types of businesses. Going forward, it need to be an essential part of the marketing plan that is being implemented. It is ideal for social media and other digital marketing initiatives to operate in tandem with one another in order to maximize the number of potential customers that are effectively reached.

1.9 How to Choose Between Digital Marketing and Social Media Marketing?

It is difficult to pick between digital marketing and social media marketing, and doing so is not recommended. Digital marketing is more effective by far. On the other hand, there are certain characteristics that will assist in selecting either one or both in a manner that will make marketing more effective and beneficial.

1.9.1 Theoretical Knowledge

There is no need for a marketing degree to work in the field of digital or social media marketing. There are entry-level roles available in each of these occupations for those who have no previous experience in marketing. On the other hand, a course that not only teaches the most recent skills in the field but also covers all areas of digital marketing is much more beneficial.

1.9.2 Personal Interests

A person's choice will determine which of the two marketing strategies or careers they choose to pursue. There is a significant amount of room for advancement in each of these areas, and in order to pursue either of these career paths, you will need to demonstrate an interest in data analysis, project management, performing experiments, testing hypotheses, and working a team.

1.9.3 Career Goals

Marketing via social media and marketing through digital platforms both provide opportunities to increase one's salary and advance one's profession. If you advance in your career, there is a greater chance that you will be given the job of managing other people and being given responsibility for the social media or digital marketing strategy of your organization.

1.10   Final Thoughts

It would be necessary for a digital marketing manager to be knowledgeable about the many digital marketing disciplines and to be able to supervise the execution of a strategy that assists the organization in accomplishing its marketing goals. However, in contrast to other marketing managers, a social media marketing manager will be responsible for establishing, executing, and iterating a company's social media strategy. Despite this, they will have a more restricted emphasis than other marketing managers. One other thing that will be required of them is that they will have understanding of the numerous marketing tactics and tools, as well as social media platforms. Become an AI-driven digital marketer today by enrolling in our PG Digital Marketing Program, which will teach you about all of the instruments, tactics, and ideas that are associated with digital marketing.

Chapter No. 02

What is social media management? Everything you need to know

When it comes to social media, a company's presence may either make or smash a brand. Posts that are scheduled appropriately have the potential to establish long-lasting relationships with the audience. The way in which customers see an organization may be altered via the use of creative images and content. The strength of social media management lies in this very aspect.

Over the course of the last several years, we have seen companies such as Wendy's, Duolingo, and others successfully garner new followers and consumers by using their inventive brand accounts. This achievement is not a coincidence. A social media marketing plan is built and maintained using a method that has been meticulously created, and all of this is a component of that method. Within the scope of this essay, we will dissect all of the moving pieces that are responsible for ensuring the seamless operation of those methods. Take use of these foundations of social media management to guide the methods that your organization uses in order to construct a presence that is worthy of being followed across the platforms that are most important.

2.1 Social media management

A continuous process that involves the creation and scheduling of content with the intention of expanding and cultivating an audience across various social media platforms is referred to as social media management. This applies to, but is not limited to the following:

- Content strategy for social media systems
- Administration of one's online reputation
- Management of the community and social programs
- Social media operations and strategies that are paid for
- Management of team members and their future growth

In addition to increasing brand exposure and keeping up with the most recent trends on the internet, the advantages of managing social media go well beyond those expectations. Building more personal interactions with target audiences at scale is made possible via the channel, which is essential. The trust, affinity, and most importantly, loyalty of a brand may be built via the rapport that is created on social media.

2.2   Evolution of social media management

There is no static definition of social media management; rather, it is constantly evolving. The tasks that are involved in maintaining a brand account are continually changing since platforms and trends are always changing. This means that the obligations are always changing. Take, for instance, the fact that the creator economy has fundamentally revolutionized the way in which we post on social media in a span of less than a few years. Conversations have moved from the public to the private sphere as a result of the proliferation of social messaging, which has resulted in more intimate relationships between individuals and the companies that they adore. It has been transformed from an awareness-focused experience into a full-funnel experience as a result of social commerce, which has altered the way business executives approach the channel. The fact that social media is driving how customers connect with companies is shown by these developments, which demonstrates that social media plays an essential role in business.

2.3   Responsibilities of a manager of social media
While social media managers are accountable for a variety of activities, including administrative and team development responsibilities, they are also responsible for devising strategies that sustain and build a social presence. Creation of content, advertising plans, career planning, and reporting on analytics are just some of the things that may be on your to-do list on any given day. To be effective in a position that is so fluid, you need a certain set of talents, which may include, but are not limited to the following:

- Cape of adjusting
- The administration
- Creative spirit
- A sense of wonder
- Methods of being critical

Social media experts are able to better handle the ever-changing requirements of this business-critical channel because to the combination of these abilities.

2.4   How to manage social media profiles
The management of social media accounts is a profession that requires both art and science. It is possible for your data to provide you with a decent sense of how to invest your resources, both in terms of money and time; yet, societal shifts occur very fast. Tomorrow, the platform that is now generating results can see a decline. If you want to be sure

that you are prepared for any obstacles that may come your way, diversifying your network approach is a solid method to do it. If your presence is well-maintained throughout the social landscape, an algorithm modification on one platform will have less of an impact on the system than if it were implemented on another site.

In situations like this, having a social media management tool is really necessary. There is a significant time investment involved in posting natively across several social media accounts. This is because it is necessary to enter into each social network manually in order to publish. Once you take into account the aspects of involvement and monitoring, it becomes more than just a full-time job. Tools like as Sprout assist firms in scaling their social activities in a sustainable manner. Workflows for publishing allow for customisation based on the network while also reducing risk. To put it another way, when your team is operating socially natively, quality control management becomes much more difficult.

Using these capabilities, you will be able to move out of the weeds and into the wider picture since they automate and complement the procedures that are already in place.

2.5 Finding your brand's target audience on social

Identifying your target audience is essential to the process of producing content that has an effect. People who fall within this category are considered to be part of the total addressable market for your brand. Your ability to develop more effective message across all of your social media sites will be enhanced if you zero in on these specific folks. By asking the following questions, you will be able to better locate and appeal to the target demographic for your brand:

- Can you tell me about your present audience?
- What specific information are they seeking for, and why are they looking for it?
- How do they get this information? Where do they go?
- What kinds of cultural events and themes do they find interesting?

Your approach to social media will be shaped by the responses you provide to these prompts, including the platforms on which you are present, the way your brand sounds online, the trends that are appealing to your audience, and the manner in which you communicate with your consumers. Understanding your audience is not a one-time activity; rather, it is an ongoing process. It is possible to maintain a mentality that prioritizes the needs of the client by asking these questions on a regular basis to both yourself and your team.

2.6 Social media content creation

The production of content is an essential component of managing across social media platforms. Even while people may log on to their preferred social networks in order to interact with their friends and family, more than one-third of them (36.3% of them) do so in order to get something to do. However, despite the fact that the competition is fierce, you may make advantage of these free minutes to establish long-lasting relationships with your audience. While you are competing for attention on social media platforms, you are not just up against direct competition but also additional components that are clamoring for attention. Other sources of information, such as media outlets, magazines, and producers, are something that marketers need to take into consideration.

Are you trying to amuse the people who are watching you? Commentary on things that are becoming viral? Is it a community? Suggestions and advice? There is a wide variety of reasons why customers decide to interact with companies on social media. In a social world that is always evolving, it is important for your company to determine where it fits in order to keep its relevance. Short-form video is the most engaging sort of in-feed social material when it comes to formats used for those types of content. TikTok's quick climb to popularity was largely responsible for its rise to prominence, and it has now expanded to all of the main social platforms in some form or another.

Short-form video is an effective method for capturing the interest of your audience without forcing them to devote a significant amount of their time to the endeavor. An approach to social media marketing that is diverse, on the other hand, takes use of all different kinds of material. Even while it could seem to be overpowering, this is really an opportunity disguised as a challenge. There are hundreds of short-form video snippets, GIFs, text pieces, and other types of content that may be created with a single live video broadcast. When it comes to social media platforms such as Instagram, Twitter, LinkedIn, and TikTok, Sprout uses its See Social Differently podcast to provide content for user-generated content.

2.7   Team member management

According to the findings of The Sprout Social IndexTM 2022, more than eighty-eight percent of marketers anticipate increasing the size of their team during the next two years.

Although this kind of development may be an incredible opportunity, it does come with a learning curve that must be overcome. Making a commitment to your own continual growth is also a necessary step in developing the potential of your team.

In order to strengthen your social media team, you should focus on developing the following four skills:

- As you go into a job that involves managing people, you will discover that you are required to speak more often on behalf of the efforts that your team is providing. In order to effectively explain the effects of your social media management strategy, it is essential to have a solid understanding of how to collect and analyze data.
- Time management is a very important skill to have while working remotely or in hybrid environments. The number of meetings that need to take place in order to put a plan into action may rapidly consume your schedule. These meetings include stand-ups, one-on-ones, project kickoffs, and all the others. Schedule certain times during which you will be concentrating on something, and be sure to do frequent audits of your meetings.
- The ability to both provide and accept feedback that is constructive is more than just a specific talent. As a superpower, it is it. An overwhelming majority of human resource executives (89%) are in agreement that

continuous feedback from peers is the key to improved business results.

- The majority of social media workers are required to remain online during times of uncertainty, brand crises, and tragedies that occur throughout the globe. When it comes to implementing preventive steps, you shouldn't wait until someone is already struggling with burnout. In order to advocate for your team, you need make sure that mental health is at the center of your talks, both during the good times and the terrible times.

2.8 Reputation management

Have you ever considered making a purchase from a business, only to discover that they have received negative feedback on the internet? Have you made the purchase that you had planned to make? On the other hand, you are not the only one. The findings of a survey conducted by Bright Local indicate that just three percent of consumers are willing to consider doing business with a company that has an average rating of two stars or lower.

The maintenance of one's reputation on social media is an essential component of social media management that is yet often neglected. Although it may not be considered one of the key tasks of a social professional, it is very necessary for the success of any and all enterprises. In the event that you are new to managing your online reputation, the following three guidelines might serve as a guide for your strategy:

2.8.1 Ask for reviews with tact

It is not necessary for you to wait for reviews to become available on their own. At other instances, all you have to do is inquire. Make contact with your most devoted customers and power users to see whether or not they would be willing to talk about their experiences with your product or services. It is imperative that you simplify the procedure as much as possible. Through the provision of a particular prompt or template, it is possible to boost consumer follow-through.

2.8.2 Respond to both the good and the bad
According to the findings of the same Bright Local poll, more than half of customers are more inclined to avoid doing business with companies who do not reply to evaluations. It might be challenging to respond to unfavorable reviews, but doing so is an effective approach to demonstrate to customers that you are aware of and value their input.

2.8.3 Be proactive about risk management
It's not always the case that feedback will arrive via direct routes. Many times, individuals may discuss your company on their personal pages without tagging or referencing your brand account. This is happening rather frequently. If you want to keep on top of the various discussions that are taking place around your company and sector, a social listening strategy may be of great assistance. In order to support an opportunity-driven brand reputation management approach that assists you in establishing long-lasting relationships with your audience, you should make use of a social listening tool such as Sprout's!

2.9   Social media management and scheduling tools
Five years ago, it was difficult to successfully manage an active social media presence using native publishing

technologies. These days, it is really difficult to do on your own. There is a greater amount of activity on social media calendars than ever before due to the fact that users are posting information, replying to customers, and managing sponsored projects. In order for businesses to meet the requirements of a contemporary social media strategy, they need to devote resources to the acquisition of social media management and scheduling tools. These gadgets are capable of more than just saving time. The following is a list of the advantages that come with using a social media management tool:

- Increased brand exposure via effective optimization of post timings, which led to enhanced performance.
- Through the consolidation of incoming communications into a single area, which allows for shorter reaction times, better engagement may be achieved.
- Improved analytics that give a more comprehensive perspective into the entire success of your social strategy.
- It is possible to improve your complete marketing technology stack by including a social media management application, which can make it simpler to connect the dots regarding the influence that social media has on your firm.

2.10   Managing a social media calendar

Your content strategy for social media should explain the main themes that guide your publication schedule and how it connects to the aims of your organization. The social media content calendar that you use gives you a more detailed view of what you are publishing and when you are posting it across all of your channels. An ideal condition for your content calendar would be one in which it could facilitate both organization and ideation. For the purpose of determining whether or not you are meeting the content mix that was defined in your plan, a bird's eye perspective of your forthcoming social media postings might be helpful.

Take, for instance, the fact that your company places a strong focus on the recruitment of excellent people. You may determine whether or not you have sufficient employer brand posts planned for the next week or month by taking a look at the content calendar that you have created for your social media accounts. Because of this exposure, it will be much simpler to determine which aspect of the text need more attention. You may utilize the Calendar Notes function of Sprout to keep track of prospective content ideas. This is a helpful hint for those who are utilizing the platform.

2.11   Paid social media ads

Worry not if you are considering whether it is more beneficial to depend on organic or sponsored social media; there is no need to make a decision between the two. Relationships with your fans that are maintained over time are supported by your organic efforts. Your advertising plan for social media, on the other hand, can assist you in reaching new consumers in a quicker and more reliable manner via the use of targeting. By combining organic and paid marketing efforts, a company can ensure that its brand remains in the forefront of the minds of both its current and potential consumers. It is much more advantageous if you are able to control them inside the same user interface. For instance, Sprout offers support for sponsored social promotion and reporting on platforms, allowing marketers to keep a close eye on how well their campaigns are doing. By doing so, you will be able to check that the money is being spent efficiently and, if it is not, you will be able to make any required modifications.

2.12 Social media community management

Despite the fact that online communities have been present for quite some time, they have never been more significant than they are right now. Take, for example, the Facebook group that Canva maintains. Canva Design Circle is home to more than 250,000 users who are looking for design guidance from their peers among other designers.

It is not necessary for the talks that are taking place inside the group to be centered on the product; nevertheless, this is not usually the case. Even if they are not linked to the product, posts have the ability to supply their team with a vital insight into the requirements of their audience.

The proliferation of communities such as these and vertical social networks has led to an increase in the number of individuals who are choosing to conduct their online interactions inside the confines of private groups. If you want to maintain a relationship with the people who make up your target audience, the most effective thing you can do is provide them with a platform where they can establish their own connections and construct a social community. A social media community that is active cannot be constructed in a single day, just like Rome. It is important to adopt a methodical and measured approach whether introducing new programs or establishing a totally new community.

In order to test drive your approach, you should begin by establishing a beta program that is exclusive to clients that are devoted to your brand and power users. When you've found your rhythm, you'll be able to increase the size of your audience.

2.13 Navigate the changing world of social media management with confidence

The insights and knowledge that are necessary for companies to understand where they fit in the cultural environment of today may be obtained via the use of social media. Maintaining an online presence is just one of the many functions that a powerful social media management plan can do. Over the course of many years to come, it may assist a brand in gaining relevance, gaining supporters, and future-proofing itself.

Taking native publishing out of the equation enables your team to access a vast array of opportunities that were previously unavailable to them. The user-friendly social media publishing tools provided by Sprout reduce the amount of manual labor required, allowing you to concentrate on enhancing your strategy and establishing connections with your clients.

Chapter No. 03

Top Social Media Sites to Consider for Your Brand in 2024

It is beneficial to have knowledge about the most prominent social media platforms that are now available, regardless of whether you are an experienced social media marketer, a marketer who is interested in transitioning into social media marketing, or a company owner who wants to take advantage of the huge potential that social media currently has. For this reason, you will be able to optimize the reach of your business, interact with the appropriate individuals, and achieve your social media objectives.

Undoubtedly, the sheer number of users on the myriad of social networking applications that are now available is not the only factor to consider. In addition to this, you should consider if the social networking site is suitable for both you and your company. Does it adhere to the image of your brand? Does that social media platform have a user base that you want to attract? Which many of social media channels are you able to maintain simultaneously?

After doing research and compiling information on the most popular social networking platforms in 2024, we made things simpler for ourselves. While some of them will sound familiar to you, others could be unfamiliar to you. We suggest that you browse through this list in order to get further information about the social media applications that might be beneficial for your company. Keep in mind that in order to have a successful brand, you do not need to be present on each and every social media platform.

Social media apps and platforms for 2024

The significance of the content to businesses and authors, in addition to the number of monthly active users, is taken into consideration when determining order on our list.

3.1 Facebook — 3.03 billion MAUs

According to Statista, Facebook is the most popular social networking site, with more than three billion users participating in its activities on a monthly basis. Facebook is used by around 37 percent of the world's population, according to this measurement. Facebook Messenger, the direct messaging program that is a spin-off of Facebook, has 931 million users that are active on a monthly basis. If you want to establish a presence on social media, Facebook is a very safe pick since more than seven million advertisers regularly market their company on Facebook, and more than 200 million companies, the majority of which are small businesses, utilize the tools that Facebook provides.

Due to the fact that practically all material forms, including text, photographs, video content, and Stories, operate very well on Facebook, getting started on Facebook cannot be more straightforward. On the other hand, the algorithm that Facebook uses gives priority to material that generates discussions and meaningful connections between individuals, particularly those that include relations with family and friends.

3.2   YouTube — 2.5 billion MAUs

On a daily basis, users of YouTube view one billion hours of videos on the site that allows them to share videos. In addition to being the second most popular social networking app, YouTube is often referred to as the second most popular search engine, behind Google, which is YouTube's parent corporation. Therefore, if you utilize videos to promote your company, you should absolutely include YouTube into your marketing approach. Here is a guide that will walk you through the process of creating a YouTube channel for your business.

3.3   WhatsApp — 2 billion MAUs

More than 180 nations are represented by users of the messaging program known as WhatsApp. WhatsApp was first used by users for the purpose of sending text messages to their closest friends and family members. WhatsApp became the medium via which individuals began connecting with companies over time. Businesses are able to give customer service and communicate updates with clients about their purchases using WhatsApp business platform. In the case of big enterprises, the WhatsApp Business API is available, while the WhatsApp Business app is designed specifically for small firms. Considering that WhatsApp is the messaging medium that is used the most, it has the potential to be an excellent customer care channel for your company.

3.4   Instagram — 2 billion MAUs

Instagram, which is a social networking site that focuses on visual content, is the ideal location to showcase your goods or services via the use of photographs or videos. The application allows users to share a broad variety of information, including live videos, photographs, movies, Stories, and Reels, among other multimedia formats. You are able to establish an Instagram business profile as a brand, which gives you access to extensive statistics on your profile and posts, as well as the capability to plan Instagram posts by using tools provided by third-party companies. Additionally, it is an excellent location to get user-generated material from your audience due to the fact that consumers commonly post content and tag certain businesses.

3.5   WeChat — 1.3 billion MAUs

The Chinese technology company Tencent, which is one of the largest in China, launched WeChat in the year 2011. WeChat, much like WhatsApp and Messenger, was first established as a chat application; however, it has now developed into an all-in-one platform. Users are able to do a variety of things, including but not limited to: shopping online, paying bills, purchasing groceries, transferring money, making bookings, booking cabs, and more.

It is safe to say that WeChat is the most widely used social networking application in China and across Asia. As a result, WeChat is an excellent option to consider if you are looking to promote your company in China, where famous social networks like as Facebook and X are prohibited. Both the official WeChat account and WeChat Moments are places where you may run advertisements. Additionally, there are a great number of influencers centered on WeChat that may assist your company in appealing to millions of Chinese customers.

3.6   TikTok — 1.05 billion MAUs

An app that allows users to share short videos is called TikTok (in China, it is called Douyin). In spite of the fact that it was just released in 2017, it has quickly become one of the most popular applications in the world and has recently surpassed Google as the most viewed website on the internet. The software TikTok gives users the ability to create and share films that are anywhere from 15 to 60 seconds in length. Additionally, the app provides users with a wide library of sound effects, music samples, and filters that can be used to improve the videos and make them more attractive.

You are able to locate films that are related to practically any passion, including lip-syncs, dancing, and challenges, as well as do-it-yourself methods and lessons on how to apply makeup. The age range of people who use TikTok in the United States is around 47.4 percent. For this reason, TikTok is an excellent social media network for your company to be present on if the population you are trying to reach is young.

3.7   Telegram — 700 million MAUs

Telegram is a free chat service that can be used on numerous devices and does not impose any restrictions on the size of the media files. The end-to-end encryption that Telegram provides for all activities, including conversations, groups, and material that is exchanged between members, is the characteristic that sets it apart from other messaging apps. Throughout the years, it has been able to attract a greater number of consumers because to its emphasis on security, particularly when WhatsApp revealed modifications to its privacy policy that would let it to share information with its parent company, Meta.

Furthermore, in addition to offering one-on-one customer service, there are a number of other ways that organizations may use Telegram. By way of illustration, companies have the ability to develop chatbots for the Telegram platform or use the channel capability of Telegram in order to broadcast messages to a maximum of 200,000 individuals.

3.8   Snapchat — 557 million MAUs

Snaps are brief films and photographs that are exchanged between friends on Snapchat. Snaps are also known as "snaps." It was the catalyst that led to the widespread adoption of the vertical video format, which later spread to other visual social media applications such as Instagram and TikTok. On the other hand, it seems that the proliferation of Instagram Stories, in particular, has hampered the development of Snapchat as well as the enthusiasm of marketers in utilizing Snapchat for their businesses in general.

Despite this, 69% of adolescents in the United States report using Snapchat. Therefore, you should think about utilizing the app if the majority of your target audience is comprised of adolescents. In the event that you are not acquainted with Snapchat, we recommend that you read our guide for beginners to Snapchat. Additionally, if you are unsure about whether Snapchat or Instagram is better for your company, we have compiled a brief comparison of the two platforms for businesses.

3.9   Kuaishou — 626 million MAUs

When compared to Douyin or TikTok, Kuaishou is a Chinese competitor. Kuaishou, much like its rivals, gives users the ability to add sound bites and stickers to photographs or videos, as well as to superimpose text on top of them. Additionally, users have the ability to record lengthier movies or live stream material to their followers on the particular site. Kuaishou is more popular among an older audience than TikTok is, particularly in rural areas of China. This is especially true in more remote areas. E-commerce income is also more important to the app than advertising money is to its overall revenue.

3.10   Qzone — 600 million MAUs
Qzone is yet another software developed by Tencent that is headquartered in China and combines social networking and blogging. It has more than 600 million users that are engaged on a subscription basis. Within the social media application, users have the ability to upload multimedia files, maintain journals, compose blogs, play games, and stream music. Users are able to connect with their friends, see a stream of updates, comment on posts, share or respond to postings, and change their cover or profile photographs, much as when they use Facebook.

3.11   Sina Weibo — 584 million MAUs
The term "Weibo" in Chinese refers to a micro-blog. Sina Corporation, a Chinese technology firm, introduced Sina Weibo, often known as Weibo, in 2009. Sina Weibo is a microblogging network that is comparable to Twitter and Instagram. Weibo allows users to publish photographs, videos, and stories; it also allows users to see trending topics; users may include hashtags in their postings; and users can use the site to send and receive instant messages.

When compared to WeChat, Sina Weibo caters to a younger population and provides material that is both more informative and more in line with current trends. In point of fact, according to The New York Times, Weibo is the place to be if you "want to go viral" in China. Additionally, Weibo enables companies to establish official and verified accounts, which enables them to connect with their followers and engage in paid advertising services.

3.12   QQ — 574 million MAUs

Tencent introduced QQ to the Chinese market in the year 1999. Prior to the introduction of WeChat, the most popular messaging app in China was QQ. QQ allows users to do a variety of things in addition to instant chatting, including decorating their avatars, watching movies, playing online games, streaming music, shopping online, blogging, and making payments among other things.

QQ is still widely used by younger people who use social media, despite the fact that WeChat has become the dominant social media platform in China. Additionally, it is used in eighty nations and is accessible in a great number of additional languages. You don't need a phone number to join up for QQ, which is one of the benefits of using this service. This appeals to younger folks who do not have mobile devices but use the desktop version of the website. QQ, on the other hand, is more popular among those who are now employed. QQ's desktop messenger is widely used because of its user-friendliness and its capacity to send files that are larger than 25 megabytes, a feature that WeChat does not permit.

3.13   X (formerly Twitter) — 556 million MAUs

X, a platform that has around 556 million monthly active users (as of January 2023), extends an invitation to a group of people who like posting about various topics, including politics, sports, entertainment, and news. What differentiates the platform that was formerly known as Twitter from the majority of other social networking sites is that it places a significant emphasis on real-time information, which includes things that are occurring and trending at the moment, and it does it in only 280 characters (140 for Japanese, Korean, and Chinese).

Twitter is used by a number of organizations as an alternative avenue for customer care. It has been reported by marketers on Twitter that Twitter is the platform where more than 80 percent of social customer support queries are made. Additionally, Salesforce refers to Twitter as the "New 1-800 Number for Customer Service for Customers." Be sure to check out our Twitter Tips for Beginners if you are just starting out on the network. When you have a firm grasp on the fundamentals, you should investigate the 20 hidden ways to use advanced search for marketing and sales respectively.

3.14   Pinterest — 445 million MAUs

Pinterest serves as a one-stop shop for finding new ideas and items, as well as for finding inspiration online. On Pinterest, users "pin" photographs that link to websites, product pages, blog entries, and other material that may be found anywhere on the internet. Pinterest's user base is seven times more likely to buy things that they have pinned, making it an excellent platform for generating traffic to your website. Fashion, beauty, home and garden, and do-it-yourself endeavors are among the most popular subjects and themes on the social site. Consequently, if your company is involved in any of those sectors, you should give serious consideration to using Pinterest marketing in order to increase the amount of exposure that your company receives.

3.15 Reddit — 430 million MAUs

Reddit has been referred to be the "front page of the internet" due to the fact that it features a variety of content, including celebrity "ask me anything" (AMA) events, in-depth discussions on specialized subjects, and current events. In April 2023, the website saw around 1.7 billion views. There are subreddits, which are essentially forums that are devoted to a certain topic, for most topics under the sun. Therefore, it is a good idea to do research to determine whether or not there are popular subreddits that your business may be a part of. Subreddits, on the other hand, have varying degrees of involvement. For instance, if your company is a beauty brand, you could benefit from joining the r/beauty subreddits.

Be conscious of the fact that the majority of subreddits do not permit self-promotion. The purpose of this endeavor is to interact with users of the different subreddits by posing and responding to questions, exchanging advice and resources, and taking part in conversations. Additionally, in addition to posting your own material on Reddit and taking part in conversations, you can also get ideas for content and advertise on the platform.

3.16 LinkedIn — 424 million MAUs

LinkedIn began as a straightforward job search engine and resume website, but it has since expanded into a professional networking platform where industry professionals can exchange information, network with one another, and create their personal brands. The platform now has around 424 million monthly active users. Additionally, it has evolved into a location where companies can identify themselves as thought leaders in their respective sectors and attract the best people. For the purpose of assisting you in expanding your LinkedIn Business Page, we have crafted a straightforward five-step method. In addition, LinkedIn provides chances for advertising, such as the capability to have tailored advertisements sent to the inboxes of users.

3.17 Twitch — 140 million MAUs

The live-streaming network Twitch caters specifically to gamers. In addition to various types of entertainment, it provides material related to video games. You have the ability to establish a channel, broadcast your games, and engage in conversation with your audience via the use of chat. Twitch has developed into a primary center for the communities who are involved in gaming and esports. The matches of a great number of professional players, teams, and tournaments are aired on this platform, which is why it is so popular. The community-driven strategy that Twitch takes is the primary factor behind its success. This method enables content producers to cultivate a devoted audience and generate revenue via subscriptions, contributions, and sponsorships.

3.18 Tumblr — 135 million MAUs

One of the most prominent social media platforms for microblogging, Tumblr has 135 million members that are active on a monthly basis. The material that users post may be submitted in a variety of forms, including text, photographs, videos, GIFs, audio samples, links, and more. Content is shared by users of the website on any and all topics, niches, and interests that can be imagined. Additionally, Tumblr gives you the ability to personalize the appearance of your blog. Due of this particular reason, a significant number of people choose to make their Tumblr account their website.

3.19 Mastodon — 1.7 million MAUs

Mastodon, a relatively young player in the social media industry, saw a meteoric rise in popularity in the latter half of 2022, going from having 300,000 members to having over 1.7 million monthly active users by the year 2023. Users are able to connect with one another via the usage of Mastodon, which is a decentralized and open-source program that enables them to build up servers. Users have the ability to make posts that are up to 5,000 characters long and include audio, video, and photos.

3.20 Bluesky — MAU unknown

Bluesky is a social network that is based on an open-source protocol and was designed to be decentralized and invite-only. Despite the fact that they have not yet disclosed their monthly active user counts to the public, the platform reached the milestone of one million members in September of 2023. Bluesky was developed by Jack Dorsey, who had previously served as the CEO of Twitter, when he was still in that position. A remarkable similarity can be seen between the platform and Dorsey's previous offering, which is also available as separate applications for iOS and android.

3.21 Be selective with your social media presence

There is no need for you to be present everywhere at the same time (Buffer is seldom active on Facebook). Therefore, regardless of the size of the social media site, you should think about whether or not the audience that your company is trying to reach is current on such platforms. Instead of producing material that is just average for five or more various platforms, it is preferable to focus on two to three sites and do really well on those sites.

Buffer is a social media scheduling tool that allows you to plan posts to many popular social networking platforms. If you want to manage several social media accounts across different platforms, you should give Buffer a try. It is completely free, and you can see what it can achieve for your company by exploring its capabilities.

Chapter No. 04

How to Check Website Traffic

It is possible that you would want to maintain track of the traffic that is coming to your own website or that of a competitor's website. Whether you are attempting to attract new followers or customers, or you are just interested in gaining a better understanding of the level of popularity that your material has, there are a variety of tools that may assist you. There are a variety of approaches that may be used from your own website; however, some of these approaches provide more of an estimate than a concrete figure. There are other approaches that are more technical and may not meet your requirements. Gaining the ability to monitor your own online traffic as well as the traffic of your rivals may be of great assistance to you in ensuring the success of your organization, regardless of the professional requirements you have.

4.1   Monitoring Traffic from Your Own Website

Your webpage's statistics may be accessed. It is fairly simple to have access to the statistics of your website if you are using a platform such as WordPress. These functions are included into the web platform to facilitate simple monitoring and maintenance, and they will provide you with an accurate picture of the traffic that is sent to your site.

- If you are using WordPress, go to the top left side of the main page and click on Dashboard. You'll find a number of other categories below it.

- Click on the My Blogs link. When you look next to the major blog that you have marked, you will see a little icon with a graph inside of it that is titled Stats. You may use it to see the total traffic that your website receives.

4.1.1 Check the number of blog post comments

Examine the total number of comments on the blog article. You may obtain a rough estimate of the number of people that visit your website by looking at the number of comments that are left on it. This is a simple and cost-free method. It should come as no surprise that not every person who views your website will leave a remark. If you are aware of this number, you will be able to more accurately estimate the amount of traffic that your website receives. On average, around one out of every 200 readers will leave a remark.

- Please go to the "comments" area of the website
- You will need to manually count the number of comments if the page does not provide a list of them
- To get a rough estimate of the number of people who have visited your page, increase the number of comments by 200 and multiply the result
- Please keep in mind that the accuracy of this procedure is not one hundred percent. Only for the purpose of providing you with a preliminary estimate, based on typical percentages, this is being done

4.1.2 Go to your homepage's video section

Take a look at the video area of your homepage. You just need to go to a video on your website and click on it in order to play it if you have incorporated YouTube or Video into your website. Both YouTube and Vimeo will display the number of views that your video has gotten; however, this is only the case if the films have been shared publicly. In the event that they are not, you will not be able to determine the amount of traffic that was passing through the website.

- If you look at the bottom right hand side of the screen, just below the video screen, you will identify a number. Your video has had a certain amount of visitors, as shown by that number.
- Please keep in mind that the number of views that are reported does not always equate to the number of views that actually occur. People who clicked on it for a short period of time and then departed are included in that figure; still, it should provide you with a general notion of the traffic that your website receives.

4.2   Monitoring Traffic Using Plugins and Websites

Make use of Google Analytics. The online traffic monitoring program known as Google Analytics is among the most widely used ones currently available. This feature enables you to monitor the path that each visitor followed in order to get at your website, which might assist you in determining how to broaden your audience.

- There are free and paid premium formats available for Google Analytics.
- A one-of-a-kind tracking number will be sent to you after you have successfully registered for Google Analytics. Through the incorporation of that code into your pages, Google will be able to monitor when your website is viewed, who visited your website, and how they discovered your page.

- When using the traffic tracker, be sure to exclude your own page views using the filtering feature. If you do not separate your hits from the usual traffic that you get, you will end up with severely skewed statistics. There is a good chance that you visit your website rather often.
- The removal of junk traffic, which may further distort your findings, is another important step that you should do.

4.2.1   Try out Alexa

Alexa is a cloud-based online information service that provides you with comprehensive data about your website. A variety of metrics, including visitors, popularity rankings, demographics reached, web speed, and more, may be monitored. Although Alexa is not free, the services it offers make it possible to get quick and thorough information while still being simple to use. Depending on the funds you have available and the requirements of your company, there are a variety of various programs available.

It is possible to use Alexa to monitor not only your own website but also the websites of your rivals. In addition, Alexa is able to provide you with suggestions that are based on the traffic history and data of your site. Utilizing these suggestions may assist you in enhancing the reach of your page and attracting a greater number of visitors to your website.

4.2.2   Keeping tabs with Compete

Comparable to Alexa is the game Compete. Compete is a tool that assists you in monitoring the traffic that comes to your website from people located in the United States. In addition to that, it provides a toolbar that enables you to promptly access the statistics of your website at any moment. Competition is not free, however the website does have a variety of membership levels to choose from. There are certain elements that are included in each plan that are meant to assist with any degree of reporting.

4.3   Tracking Competitors' Websites

Determine your rivals in the market. Monitoring the traffic that comes to your own website is essential; nevertheless, if you really want to develop your webpage, you need also keep an eye on the websites that are competing with you. In the future, it will be helpful for you to make judgments about your own webpage if you are aware of the ways in which a competitor's website is different from your own and how he communicates with his audience. Conduct a search using a variety of internet search engines for the most important keywords associated with your site. This can assist you in gaining a comprehensive grasp of the websites that your target audience often visits in addition to your own. It is quite probable that the top ten websites are your most significant rivals.

4.3.1   Evaluate their websites

Conduct a review of their websites. In the event that your rivals are reaping the benefits of increased web traffic, it may be attributed to either the superior design of their websites or the more efficient optimization of search engine queries. While you are comparing your website to the sites of your rivals, you should also attempt to figure out what you might do differently to capitalize on some of the success that they have achieved.

4.3.2 Utilize web traffic monitoring tools

Utilize technologies that monitor the traffic on the web. Although you may use some of the analytical tools to monitor your own website traffic, you can also use some of these services to monitor the websites of your rivals. Compare the evaluations of each monitoring tool, and look for the tools that provide the services that are the most accurate and of the highest quality. Read evaluations written by other users on the internet, or experiment with a variety of tools to determine which ones are the most effective for you. Free trials are available on a number of premium membership websites, while others are completely free to access.

Chapter No. 05

How to use social listening to boost website traffic

Because we live in a digital era, social media has developed into an essential component of our everyday lives. In addition to this, it has developed into an indispensable instrument for businesses who are wanting to increase the amount of traffic that visits their websites. The practice of social listening is among the most efficient methods for accomplishing this goal. A method known as social listening involves monitoring several social media sites in order to identify any mentions of your company, goods, or sector. Companies are able to enhance their online presence and increase the amount of traffic that visits their website by using social listening, which allows them to acquire vital insights about their target demographic. In the following paragraphs, we will go over the advantages of social listening as well as the ways in which it may be used to increase website traffic.

5.1   Understanding social listening and its benefits

First and foremost, in order to use social listening to increase website traffic, one must first get an understanding of it. A method known as social listening involves monitoring several social media sites in order to identify any mentions of your company, goods, or sector. Companies may enhance their online presence and increase the amount of traffic that visits their website by doing so, which allows them to gather vital insights about their target audience and utilize those insights to better their strategies.

There are a great many advantages to engaging in social listening. In the first place, it gives businesses the ability to comprehend what their intended audience is saying about them on social media. With the use of this information, the company may determine the areas in which it can make improvements and formulate adjustments that will connect with their target audience. In addition, social listening may assist businesses in recognizing trends in their respective industries, maintaining their competitive edge, and making well-informed choices on their marketing plans.

The opportunity to communicate with your audience on a more personal level is yet another advantage that comes with social listening for businesses. Companies have the ability to strengthen their connections with their audience and boost their devotion to their brand by acknowledging and reacting to comments, questions, and criticism. In general, social listening is an indispensable instrument for businesses that want to increase the amount of traffic that visits their websites and enhance their visibility on the internet. It is possible to make educated judgments that will result in a rise in the amount of traffic that visits your website and, eventually, an increase in your bottom line if you have a thorough grasp of what your target audience is saying about your business.

5.2   Identifying your target audience through social listening

When it comes to leveraging social listening to increase website traffic, one of the most important steps is to determine who your target audience specifically is. Companies are able to monitor and analyze mentions of their brand, goods, or sector on social media platforms via the use of social listening, which may give them with useful insights about their target audience. When businesses have a clear grasp of their target demographic, they are better able to adjust their marketing strategy and online presence to have a greater impact on reaching and engaging with that particular set of individuals.

Analysis of the demographics of the individuals who are referencing your brand on social media is one method that may be used to determine who your target audience is via the use of social listening practices. A person's age, gender, location, and hobbies are all examples of this kind of information. By doing so, you may have a better understanding of the individuals who are already engaged in your business and the kinds of material that connect with them.

Using social listening, you can also determine your target audience by evaluating the sentiment of the mentions of your business. This is yet another method using social listening. You will have a better understanding of how people feel about your brand and what they cherish as a result of this. This information may be used to develop messages and campaigns that are congruent with their beliefs, which will assist you in establishing a stronger connection with them.

In general, determining your target audience via social listening may give you with useful information that can assist you in tailoring your online presence and marketing methods to better reach and interact with that particular set of individuals. You will finally be able to improve the amount of visitors that visits your website and your bottom line as a result of this.

5.3   Tracking and analyzing mentions of your brand on social media

A significant component of social listening is the monitoring and analysis of mentions of your business on various social media platforms. Through the use of this technology, businesses are able to monitor and gather data on the numerous social media channels on which their brand is being discussed. By using this information, one may not only recognize patterns and trends, but also get vital insights on the audience that they are trying to reach.

A number of different tools and pieces of software are available for businesses to use in order to monitor and analyze mentions of their brand on social media platforms. With the use of these tools, businesses are able to establish hashtags and keywords that are associated with their brand, goods, or sector. The program, after it has been configured, will gather data on all instances in which certain hashtags and phrases are used, and it will then give a comprehensive analysis of the findings.

Information like as the number of mentions, the mood of the mention, the demographics of the person who mentioned the brand, and the platform where the mention happened may all be included in the analysis that is offered by these tools. It is possible to utilize this information to recognize patterns and trends, as well as to make educated judgments on how to enhance the internet presence and marketing methods. Firms may enhance their online presence, bring more visitors to their website, and eventually raise their bottom line by watching and analyzing mentions of their brand on social media. This allows the firms to obtain important insights into their target audience and utilize the knowledge about their target audience to improve their online presence.

5.4   Using social listening to identify industry trends and stay competitive

One other essential component of the plan is the use of social listening in order to recognize trends in the market and maintain a competitive edge. Companies are able to monitor and gather data on what is being said about their sector as well as their rivals on social media via the practice of social listening. It is possible to utilize this information to recognize patterns and trends in the industry, as well as to acquire useful insights into what their rivals are doing well and where they may increase their performance.

Through the monitoring of industry-related hashtags and keywords, businesses are able to maintain a state of awareness about the most recent trends, goods, and services. In order to design new goods, services, and marketing tactics that are in line with the trends that are currently occurring, this knowledge may be used. A further benefit of monitoring what people say about their competition is that it may give useful insights into what they are doing well and what they can do better.

One more method of use social listening to maintain a competitive edge is to discover influential individuals within your sector. Individuals who are regarded as authorities in their respective fields and who have a sizable following on social media are referred to as influencers. Companies are able to learn about the most recent trends in their field and uncover prospective collaborations by watching what they say and connect with one other.

All things considered, the use of social listening as a means of recognizing trends in the market and maintaining a competitive edge may provide significant data that can assist businesses in enhancing their online presence, attracting more visitors to their website, and eventually boosting their bottom line. Companies are able to engage in informed decision-making that will assist them in remaining ahead of the competition if they remain educated about the most recent trends and what their rivals are doing.

5.5   Engaging with your audience through social listening

To effectively use social listening to increase website traffic, one of the most important steps is to engage with your audience via social listening. Not only does social listening enable businesses to keep track of what is being said about them on social media, but it also enables them to interact with their audience in real time. Responding to comments, messages, and direct mentions of your company, goods, or sector on social media sites is one way to accomplish this goal.

Through active participation with their audience, businesses have the opportunity to cultivate connections and earn the trust of their intended audience. Providing replies that are both useful and relevant to comments and messages, as well as making proactive efforts to reach out to prospective consumers, are both ways in which this may be accomplished. Companies may also uncover frequent pain points or problems that come up by connecting with their audience and then using that knowledge to better their goods and services. This is made possible by the engagement of the audience.

A rise in brand recognition and an increase in the amount of traffic that visits your website may both be achieved via engagement with your audience. Through the act of replying to comments, businesses have the ability to raise the exposure of their brand on social media, which in turn may result in an increased number of individuals being aware of their brand and visiting their website. In general, one of the most important aspects of successfully using the technique to increase website traffic is to actively engage with your audience via social listening. Businesses have the ability to boost their brand recognition and increase the amount of traffic that visits their website by cultivating connections with their target audience and developing trust with them. This, in turn, will eventually improve their bottom line.

5.6 Measuring the impact of social listening on website traffic

One of the most critical steps in establishing whether or not the approach is successful is to measure the influence that social listening has on the traffic that is visiting the website. Businesses are able to monitor and gather data on what is being said about them on social media platforms via the practice of social listening. They can then utilize this knowledge to increase the amount of traffic that visits their website. Nevertheless, it is essential to monitor and assess the results of these efforts in order to ascertain whether or not they are producing the consequences that were intended.

There are a few different approaches to determining how much of an influence social listening has on website traffic. Recording the amount of visitors to a website that originate from social media platforms is one approach. This is something that can be accomplished via the use of technologies such as Google Analytics, which gives businesses the ability to see the amount of visits to their website as well as the origin of those visitors. Companies are able to identify whether or not their social listening efforts are resulting in an increase in the amount of traffic that is sent to their website by monitoring the number of visits that originate from social media.

The amount of times your business is mentioned on social media is another method that can be used to evaluate the effect that social listening has on the traffic that is sent to your website. Using software such as mention or Hootsuite, which enable businesses to monitor mentions of their brand, goods, or industry on social media, is one way to accomplish this goal. Companies are able to identify whether or not their social listening activities are increasing brand awareness and leading to an increase in the number of individuals finding their brand and visiting their website by monitoring the number of mentions from their audience.

When it comes to establishing the efficacy of the plan, one of the most crucial steps is to measure the influence that social listening has on the traffic that is generated by the website. Companies are able to evaluate whether or not they are increasing the amount of traffic that visits their website by monitoring and evaluating the effect of their social listening activities. If they are, they can then make modifications as necessary to enhance their results.

5.7   Utilizing social listening tools and software

One of the most important aspects of adopting social listening to increase website traffic is making use of the many tools and technologies available for social listening. Companies are able to monitor and gather data on what is being said about them on social media by using social listening tools and software. They can then utilize this information to generate more visitors to their website.

There is a wide selection of social listening software and tools available, each of which has its unique set of capabilities and features. Tools like as Hootsuite, Mention, and Brand24 are examples of well-known social listening applications. With the use of these tools, businesses are able to monitor mentions of their brand, goods, or sector on social media and interact with their audience in real time.

The influence of social listening on website traffic and other metrics may also be measured by some social listening technologies. These platforms provide information on website visits, mentions, and overall engagement, which allows for the measurement of the impact of social listening. The capability of social listening technologies to filter and make sense of the data that is gathered is another feature of these tools. Some systems are able to categorize mentions according to sentiment, themes, and geography, and they may even give insights on the techniques that rivals are doing.

In general, one of the most significant steps in using social listening to increase website traffic is to make use of the many tools and technologies available for social listening. By using these tools to monitor and gather data on what is being said about your company on social media, businesses have the opportunity to obtain useful insights and utilize that knowledge to drive more visitors to their website? It is essential to determine which tool works best for your particular requirements and financial constraints.

5.8   Integrating social listening with other digital marketing strategies

It is crucial for businesses who want to increase website traffic and achieve outcomes to include social listening into their digital marketing plans in addition to other digital marketing methods. It is possible to get significant insights into the behavior, preferences, and interests of customers via social listening, which may then be used to influence and improve other digital marketing efforts.

Through the use of search engine optimization (SEO), social listening may be integrated with other digital marketing methods. It is possible to get insight into the keywords and phrases that people are using to search for items or services similar to yours via social listening. This information may assist you in optimizing your website for those keywords, which in turn can boost your performance in search engine rankings.

The use of email marketing is yet another method that may be used to incorporate social listening into other digital marketing techniques. Through social listening, you may get insights into the material that connects with your audience, which will enable you to build email campaigns that are more focused and successful. With the help of social listening, content marketing tactics may be informed and supported. This is accomplished by determining which subjects are currently popular and by encouraging interaction among your audience. It is possible for you to provide material that is in line with these subjects, so providing your audience with an experience that is more relevant and interesting. In addition, social listening may be used to enhance advertising initiatives by giving information on the channels, timing, and targeting that are most effective for your audience.

In general, combining social listening with other digital marketing methods may offer businesses with a more comprehensive insight of their audience and enable them to develop campaigns that are more successful, targeted, and that deliver results. It is essential to keep in mind that social listening is not a strategy that can be used on its own; rather, it is a strategy that can be used in conjunction with other strategies to get useful data that can be used to improve your overall marketing efforts.

5.9   Best practices for conducting social listening campaigns

Conducting social listening campaigns is a key step in adopting social listening to enhance website traffic. On the other hand, in order to guarantee that your efforts are successful, there are a few best practices that you should keep in mind. Before anything else, it is essential to have a crystal clear understanding of the aims and objectives that you have for the social listening campaign. This will guarantee that you are gathering and analyzing the appropriate data, as well as that you are able to analyze the effect that your campaign has had on the traffic to your website and other metrics.

The next step is to devise a method for the collection and examination of pertinent information. Included in this is the process of determining which keywords, hashtags, and mentions are pertinent to monitor, as well as the process of setting up alerts to tell you whenever new data is received. In addition, you should provide a method for evaluating and understanding the data, such as classifying mentions according to the emotion, the subject matter, or the location associated with them.

The engagement of your audience is yet another essential component of social listening campaigns that you should consider doing. In this context, "responding to customer inquiries and complaints in a timely manner" refers to the act of finding and interacting with influential individuals within your sector. In addition, it is essential to bear in mind the ethical and legal aspects that are involved in social listening. These include the protection of personal information and the guarantee that your campaigns are in accordance with the applicable laws and regulations. As a final step, it is essential to monitor and measure the impact that your social listening campaign has on the traffic that your website receives as well as other metrics in order to assess how successful your efforts have been. In summary, doing social listening campaigns successfully entails having clear objectives, developing a method for gathering and analyzing data, connecting with your audience, being mindful of ethical and legal implications, and routinely assessing and monitoring the outcomes. Your social listening efforts will be more likely to be successful and provide results for your company if you adhere to these best practices and make sure they are implemented.

5.10   Companies successfully using social listening to increase website traffic

There have been a great number of businesses that have been able to effectively enhance website traffic by using social listening. A few instances of how they accomplished this are as follows:

- A retail apparel firm used social listening in order to monitor discussions of their brand as well as mentions of their rivals on social media. Through the analysis of the data, they were able to determine where there were gaps in their product offers and make adjustments to their inventory in order to better satisfy the requirements of their customers. This led to a rise in the number of sales and visitors to the website.
- A corporation that specializes in technology engaged in social listening in order to monitor discussions pertaining to their sector and to recognize developing trends. They were successful in increasing the amount of website traffic and the number of leads they generated by keeping ahead of the curve and implementing these trends into their marketing strategy and by putting them into their website.
- A restaurant chain used social listening in order to monitor the feelings of its patrons and uncover the most often voiced grievances. As a result of resolving these

difficulties and making modifications to their menu as well as their customer service, they were able to increase the level of pleasure experienced by their customers and attract more customers to their website.

- A travel firm engaged in social listening in order to determine the most popular vacation locations and to develop marketing strategies that were specifically targeted. They were successful in increasing the amount of internet traffic and reservations on their website by developing content and promotions that were matched with these places.

These are just a few instances of how businesses may effectively employ social listening to boost the amount of traffic that visits their websites. Companies have the ability to generate outcomes and enhance website traffic by monitoring and analyzing discussions that take place on social media platforms, determining the requirements and preferences of their customers, and using this knowledge to influence decisions about their websites and marketing tactics.

5.11   Conclusion

The practice of social listening is a powerful tool that can assist businesses in increasing website traffic. It does this by monitoring and analyzing conversations that take place on social media platforms, determining the requirements and preferences of customers, and utilizing this information to form marketing and website strategies. Companies should first define clear goals and objectives for their campaigns and build a strategy for gathering and evaluating data before attempting to employ social listening to increase the amount of traffic that visits their websites. Included in this is the process of determining which keywords, hashtags, and mentions are pertinent to monitor, as well as the process of setting up alerts to tell you whenever new data is received. A strategy for evaluating and understanding the data should also be established by businesses. This process might include classifying mentions according to the sentiment, subject, or location of the mentions.

Interacting with your audience is another essential component of utilizing social listening to increase the amount of traffic that visits your website. In this context, "responding to customer inquiries and complaints in a timely manner" refers to the act of finding and interacting with influential individuals within your sector. In addition, it is essential to bear in mind the ethical and legal aspects that are involved in social listening. These include the protection of personal information and the guarantee that your campaigns are in accordance with the applicable laws and regulations.

As a final step, it is essential to monitor and measure the impact that your social listening campaign has on the traffic that your website receives as well as other metrics in order to assess how successful your efforts have been. When businesses adhere to these best practices, they are able to employ social listening to boost the amount of traffic that visits their websites and generate results for their company.

Chapter No. 06

Online Tools to Increase Website Traffic

Is it possible that you have ever pondered to yourself, "I am content with the amount of traffic that I have received to my website?" There is no more that I need." Oh, no! Obviously, that is not the case. You never stop wanting more. Despite the fact that you are receiving a satisfactory amount of traffic to your website (and congratulations on that), there is always space for optimization. If you are having trouble obtaining some solid numbers, there are surely a variety of choices available to you that you may pursue. In any case, you shouldn't be content with the current situation you're in.

If you want your company to be successful, having a website that receives a lot of traffic is essential. There is nothing else that really matters if there is no traffic. In order to improve your chances of converting visitors into customers, you need to attract people to your website and encourage them to stay.

We are going to be concentrating on it today. Website traffic is the topic of discussion today! As a result of the abundance of strategies and tools that are now available, you will be able to enhance the total flow of visitors that visits your website. When it comes to your traffic, you have a lot of alternatives right at your disposal, ranging from attracting new people to retargeting past visitors. Here is a list of our top ten recommendations for technologies that may help enhance website traffic.

6.1   Linktree

The inability to add clickable links to posts is the one downside that everyone complains about, despite the fact that Instagram has become an invaluable resource for a great number of ecommerce firms and content providers. It may be really frustrating when you have just published material that you are trying to promote, but you only have one link available to utilize on your bio page. It is possible to update it whenever you get new material; however, this is not always the best solution since individuals may check older posts and prefer to view that content rather than the most recent post content (for example).

In this situation, Linktree is a great tool! With this, you will be able to generate an optimized link that you can include into your bio and which will then connect to a number of other sites. You have complete control over your Linktree link; you are free to add any links you choose, organize them in any order you choose, and quickly change them. Exist a brand-new product? Create a link to it! Can you upload a fresh video? Create a link to it! Is there a new post on the blog? Create a link to it! It is clear to you now.

Make it simple for your Instagram audience to visit your website by generating your own Linktree link and include it in your Instagram bio. This will eliminate the need for you to rely on the hope that your audience will find their way to your website. They are able to access any of your material with only a few clicks, which is guaranteed to ensure that you have a good increase in traffic.

6.2   SEMRush

Websites continue to place a significant emphasis on organic traffic, and SEMRush can assist you in optimizing your content and keywords in order to get a better ranking on search engine results pages and attract a greater volume of organic traffic to your website. In particular, we are really impressed with their keyword research tools, which will enable you to locate terms that will be simpler to rank for overall. In addition to doing keyword research, SEMRush also provides assistance with sponsored traffic, to name just one of its many other capabilities. To be more specific, it is one of the most comprehensive SEO tools currently available, and it is also one of our favorites. Not only should you monitor your own website, but you should also monitor the websites of your rivals to see what they are ranking for and to determine whether or not there are any possibilities for you to target yourself with unique keywords.

People continue to use search engines like Google as their primary method of looking for new items and information. With the assistance of SEMRush, you can ensure that your website is correctly optimized for search engines, which is something that is in your best interest. What is the end result? On a consistent basis, a significant increase in the amount of organic traffic that visits your website.

6.3   MailerLite

Email marketing is still a popular method for engaging your audience, and when it is done correctly, it is an excellent way to improve the amount of visitors that visits your website. When it comes to email inboxes, you encounter a great deal of rivalry; nonetheless, using a tool such as

MailerLite is an excellent strategy to assist your business in standing out from the crowd.

MailerLite is an excellent email marketing software that enables businesses to simply create emails that have a very attractive appearance and that people will really want to read and look at. Not only does its drag-and-drop builder make it feasible for any company to send interesting emails, but it also eliminates the need for a graphic designer or programming experience. Another reason why we like this tool is that it offers a wide range of excellent automation capabilities and can easily be integrated with many of the most popular online platforms and services, such as Shopify, WordPress, Optin Monster, Square Space, and many more.

There are a few examples of new freebies, new items, and fresh content that should be highlighted in email campaigns that you should schedule. Make advantage of their A/B testing functionality to experiment with different subject lines, calls to action (CTAs), graphics, and other elements in order to determine what motivates your audience to click on your content.

6.4   Adroll

Increasing the amount of people who visit your website may be accomplished via purchased traffic, which is, of course, a wonderful approach to do it. We have previously addressed organic traffic. Using Adroll, it is simple to target new prospective customers as well as retarget current customers or site users. Adroll also makes it possible to target prospects. Their retargeting advertisements are particularly amazing to us. You will have the highest chance of those people actually converting if you use retargeting, which is one of the finest strategies to generate relevant traffic to your website. In fact, it will offer you a probability that is seventy percent higher than the average. Adroll gives you the ability to create simple retargeted advertisements as well as dynamic advertisements that are depending on the content that a visitor views on your website.

The best part is that Adroll provides you with a large number of placement possibilities for your advertisements, which include placement on search engines, websites, and social media platforms. This gives you the ability to target your audience nearly anyplace they find themselves online, which is a very strong ability to have!

6.5   Hootsuite

A significant number of websites rely heavily on social media as a source of traffic. In point of fact, we strongly suggest that you review your analytics to determine the origin destination of the bulk of your visitors. What are some of the most important sources that you use? If not, there is the possibility that it will be. If this is the case, it would be wise to direct a significant portion of your digital marketing efforts at it. Whatever the case may be, Hootsuite will assist you in making it happen.

One of the most widely used social media scheduling apps is Hootsuite, and there is a solid reason for its popularity. The scheduling of postings for social media platforms such as Facebook, Instagram, Twitter, LinkedIn, Pinterest, and even YouTube is simplified with this tool. You may schedule a single post at a time, or you can utilize their bulk scheduling feature to coordinate the scheduling of hundreds of posts all at once. Additionally, we are impressed by the fact that they provide a Google Chrome plugin that enables you to plan information that you discover while you are surfing the internet. They make it quite simple to ensure that your social media channels are always stocked with informative material that will direct users to your website. Utilize it to your advantage!

6.6   Filmora

Video marketing continues to be quite popular and is an excellent method for generating a significant amount of website traffic. In point of fact, studies have shown that marketers that depend on video get an average of 41% more traffic from search engines than those who do not engage in any kind of video marketing. It is common knowledge that video is an excellent medium; nevertheless, it is also one of the most challenging forms of material to create.

Instead of using the services of a group of people to produce your video material, you may depend on a program such as Filmora and generate films on your own! Additionally, they provide a large number of filters, media, and audio clips that may be used by users, and their video editing program is simple enough for anybody to use. You are going to need a product such as Filmora to assist you in your video marketing endeavors if you are thinking about taking them seriously. If you already have expertise editing videos, you will find that using this tool makes it much simpler (and therefore more expedient) for you to generate high-quality material that you can use on your website as well as on your social media channels.

6.7 BuzzSumo

There is another strategy for attracting visitors that you probably already know about and are doing, and that is content marketing. When you have high-quality content, more people will visit your website. The important phrase here is? Superiority. Not only does the information need to be of high quality in terms of clarity, but the subject matter itself has to be intriguing and engaging in order to pique the attention of users and encourage them to read it, comment on it, and share it.

BuzzSumo makes it simpler for marketers to determine what material is currently trending, which may have a significant impact on the development of strategy. Are you going to be publishing a series of blog pieces on marketing using social media? Do a search on BuzzSumo for the phrase to find out which pieces of content are the most popular and successful ones related to that topic. In the process of creating your own material, this might serve as a useful guide. In addition, you can use this tool to locate relevant influencers with whom you may be able to contact and have them promote your material, which is yet another fantastic method for increasing the amount of traffic that you get. In addition to making things very simple, BuzzSumo will save you a significant amount of time by providing you with all of the top results in just a few clicks.

6.8 Stamped.io

The first thing that usually comes to mind when you think of product evaluations is the potential for them to assist you in increasing your sales. This is unquestionably accurate; but, did you realize that they may also assist you in increasing the amount of visitors that visits your website?

Utilizing a service like as Stamped may assist you in not just collecting reviews but also making good use of them to assist you in achieving a variety of marketing objectives, including boosting traffic.

Through the use of Stamped, you will have an easier time adding reviews right into product pages. When you have material that is both fresh and updated, you are sending a message to Google and other search engines that your content is new (and hence not out of date or relevant). Because of this, it may get a better ranking, which may lead to an increase in the amount of organic traffic. A further advantage that can be beneficial to your search engine optimization is that your reviews may also assist you in ranking keywords.

In terms of collecting your reviews, Stamped also makes it simple and straightforward for your users to provide feedback, which will enhance the likelihood that your consumers will provide you with a review at some point in the future. All of the leading e-commerce systems, such as Shopify, Woocommerce, Big Commerce, and Magento, are also compatible with their integration abilities. Stamped is a program that makes it simple for you to take use of user reviews and takes care of all the laborious work for you. If you own an online business, you certainly must take advantage of customer reviews.

6.9   Alexa

Please, Alexa, bring me more customers! Her command is to fulfill your request. To put it another way, not precisely. However, near! You will be able to improve the traffic that comes to your website with the assistance of Alexa, which is a technology that was built by Amazon. There is a lot of work that Alexa performs that is typical of SEO, but one element in particular that we particularly appreciate is the 'upstream sites' option. This feature helps you understand your competition by displaying where their site visitors originate from before arriving on their website. In this way, you will have a solid picture of where their efforts are concentrated and how they are paying off. It is possible that the bulk of the traffic comes from websites such as Google, social media, or other content websites.

With the aid of this information, you can better direct your content strategy. In the event that social media is doing exceptionally well for your rival, for instance, you are aware that there is the possibility that it will also perform exceptionally well for you. We are always really grateful for the fact that Alexa is a wonderful tool that is very simple to use.

6.10 Aimtell

Last but not least, it is imperative that you do not overlook the possibility of retargeting the visitors to your website via the use of web push notifications. These visitors have already shown an early interest in your business, which makes them far more likely to convert (as was indicated previously).

By using web push, it is possible to easily send tailored campaigns that are sent quickly to mobile devices as well as desktop computers. It is important to divide your audience into different groups and then retarget them based on the activities they do on your website and where they are in the buyer's journey. With web push, you have a number of chances for automation, one of which is retargeting abandoned carts, which is an excellent strategy that will enhance both your traffic and your sales. The fact that push notifications are known to have some of the highest click through rates makes them an excellent choice for any company that is wanting to improve the amount of traffic that visits their website. Web push alerts may be beneficial to businesses of all sizes and types, including those who operate e-commerce stores, blogs, travel agencies, and everything in between.

6.11 Conclusion

Although there are millions of websites on the Internet nowadays, this does not imply that you have no influence over the amount of traffic that visits your website. You can choose how much traffic you get or how little traffic you receive. You will be able to target (and retarget) visitors with the assistance of these ten tools for increasing website traffic, which will ultimately result in the traffic statistics that you are looking for.

You have a multitude of opportunities to boost the amount of traffic that visits your website. These opportunities include enhancing your search engine optimization (SEO) and ranking on search engines, optimizing your Instagram profile, posting product reviews, running smart advertisements, sending email campaigns, leveraging web push, and many more. The only question that remains is, what exactly are you holding out for? It is time to begin increasing your traffic!

Chapter No. 07

Importance of Website Traffic in Your Business?

When it comes to establishing credibility and trustworthiness for your business in this digital age, there are a lot of ways and strategies that can help build all of those things, and one of them is having a website. It is an easy way to reach both current and potential customers and consistently engage them by providing detailed information about your business, brand, products, services, advocacies, etc. That's why having a website is deemed necessary for every business because of its unquestionable contributions to the eminence of small to large businesses from different industries.

7.1   What is Website Traffic?

Let's say you have a good web design with responsive features and excellent user experience, but only a few know about it and your website seldom gets any visits. It wouldn't really serve its purpose, right? This is where website traffic comes in.

Website traffic is the number or volume of users visiting your website. It is often used as a metric for businesses to determine their success and effectiveness in calling the attention of a wider scope of the audience into their brand online. This means the more people visit your website, the more potential customers you will be able to engage, allowing an increase in conversion rates, sales, brand awareness, lead generation, and more for your business. A consistent increase in website traffic shows that your business is also gradually growing, reaching more people, and is adding opportunities to expand and improve your products and services.

7.2   Why is Website Traffic Important?

With what was mentioned above, to say the least, website traffic is important because it helps your business grow, but that's not really enough to emphasize its importance, isn't it? So to help you better understand, let's look at these factors that make up the importance of website traffic in your business and how each one works to bring quality traffic that benefits the business in the long run.

7.3   Website Conversion Rate

Conversion rate is the percentage of visitors that completed a desired or intended goal on your website. For example, customers who proceeded to make a purchase signed up for newsletter subscriptions, filled out a form for inquiries, etc. This signifies that the visitor is expressing interest in your product or service and are qualified leads that bring quality website traffic, resulting in the increase of conversion rate for your business. But do keep in mind that the increase in numbers doesn't always necessarily mean that everything is going well. You have to see to it that you are not just focused on how high the number of visitors is, rather the quality of leads you can drive to your website.

7.4   Types of Website Traffic

In understanding the importance of website traffic, you have to know what type of website traffic comes in and which one is found to be the most effective in turning visitors into customers.

7.4.1 Organic Traffic

Organic traffic consists of people who found your website through search engines. It is scalable, which means that the more marketing efforts you put in, the greater return on investment you will have in the long run. You can increase your organic traffic through SEO (search engine optimization). This will enable your website to grow its online visibility and improve its rank on search results.

7.4.2 Paid Traffic

This is the type of traffic you get from people who visit your website after clicking on an ad you paid for, such as Google Ads or any advertising. Paid traffic can help your website appear on search queries and improve brand awareness, generating quality traffic for your business.

7.4.3 Direct Traffic

People who visit your website directly into their browser are considered direct traffic because they are already familiar with your brand and some may even be repeat visitors or customers. Marketing your brand offline such as distributing flyers or brochures that indicate your website address can help boost direct traffic to your website. However, this type of traffic may be the least effective one because it is not as scalable as the others.

7.4.4 Referral Traffic

Referral traffic consists of people who visit your website through external links. For example, upon reading a blog article, you will find texts with hyperlinks that tell you to click it, then you are led to another page that's relevant to the one you previously visited. You can simply increase referral traffic using links. So the more links you provide, the better chances you have in leading people to follow the links that get to your website. But take note that it will be more effective if you include links on popular and credible sources because people will see that you take giving information seriously, and you are not only after selling your products to them.

7.4.5   Social Traffic
These are people who visit your website by clicking on the link that is included in a post on social media. If your business has a big following community on social media platforms, it will be easier to gather social traffic to your website. It is also scalable, so with the right marketing efforts, you will be able to get good returns. A tip for you is to engage and build a relationship with your audience on social media that will result in a strong following community for your business.

7.4.6   Your Brand Identity
People tend to keep buying products that they have already tried and avail of services that give a good experience for them. How you present your brand identity affects the way potential and current customers see your business. Having repeat customers is a good indication that you are doing something right and they are actually satisfied with your products and services. The more repeat customers you have, the more chances you have of driving qualified traffic to your website.

7.4.7   Your Marketing Efforts
Your marketing efforts play a big role in the website traffic of your business. The increase of website traffic and its quality depend on your ability to draw attention from the

right audience. Remember that your goal shouldn't be to simply drive traffic that's focused on the number of visitors itself because it will be pointless if they are not converted into customers.

7.5   The Quality of Traffic

The website traffic that your business has only becomes worthwhile when you can drive good quality traffic. An increase in traffic is good, but it will not always guarantee that your conversion rate is at a satisfactory state. At times, people will just come and visit your website without proceeding to take action. It all boils down to having an effective digital marketing strategy to back you up and help market your brand to the right audience that will make up the quality of traffic your website needs.

7.6   Why are websites a good marketing strategy?

Your website is a piece of online real estate that you own. It can stand the test of time versus a social media profile that can get shut down because you failed to follow a rule you didn't even know about. Now, all your effort and leads are gone! This isn't just about making money or getting more engagement. More website traffic in the long run can expand your product lines, help you hire more employees, open new locations, invest in research to develop more amazing services and products, and ultimately grow your business.

But a website is only a good marketing strategy to grow your business if it allows the visitor to find what they're looking for as quickly as possible. Your homepage is the first touch point potential customers have with you. This could be your only opportunity to capture their interest in what you're offering.

Marcus Sheridan, in his book They Ask, You Answer says it best:

"What are your buyers thinking the moment they land on your website? It comes down to this: 'Can (your company) solve my problem (need) or not?'

That's it. That's what is on their minds.

Therefore, the headline of your homepage - as well as just about any other page on your site - should lead with your visitor's primary problems, needs, questions, or worries in their words. Only afterward can you begin to introduce your company, what value you can provide, how you can address their problems and/or answer their questions, and so on."

Your website should answer people's questions and be educational. The ultimate goal of your website is to get the visitor to page 2. In other words, tell them what to do next and capture their information so that you can continue to nurture them as part of your business growth strategy.

7.7 What is considered good website traffic?
The larger the number of visitors to your website the better!

But not all traffic is good traffic, so you also need to focus on increasing the quality of your website traffic through SEO and quality content.

7.8 How much website traffic do you need to grow your business?

This comes down to a simple, yet sophisticated calculation. You need to have insight into the costs and expenses your business has, and how much an average customer is worth. When you know how much revenue you need (set goals) then you can work backwards to calculate how much website traffic you'll need to reach those goals. Basically you're looking at your end goal and planning backwards from there.

7.8.1 Fictitious Business Example:

- Your "Cupcake Business" is up and running.
- Your business needs $5,000 a month to maintain your current budget.
- Each customer is worth $30 (they generally buy 12 cupcakes a month at $2.50 a cupcake).
- You will need to sell 2,000 cupcakes a month. Each customer on average buys 12 cupcakes a month, then you need 166.66 customers each month.
- Working backwards, on a low average...100 website visitors converts to 1 lead. At a 1% conversion rate from a lead to a customer, you'll need 100 leads to get 1 new customer. To meet your goal of 166.66 customers, it looks like you will need to attract 1,666,666 website visitors. Phew, that seems like a lot of work.
- Keep in mind that the low conversion percentage of 1% is a conservative baseline, but businesses using online marketing strategies are seeing an increase in their conversion rates.
- If you increased your visitor to lead conversion rate to 2% and your lead to customer rate to 4% with better

qualified traffic and leads, you just decreased your total website traffic goal to 208,325. That's a decrease of 87.5% - Wow!

Website traffic is not the only thing your business needs, and depending on your industry and market, you need to keep this in mind. But your website can play a big part in your business's success!

7.9   Is website traffic more important than sales?

Both website traffic and sales are essential to a business growth strategy. However, having a lot of website visitors won't do you any good if they aren't buying your products or services.   When you can increase the quality of the website traffic and visits to your site, you're also increasing your conversion numbers and this in turn decreases the number of new website visitors you need to maintain your business goals. Keeping in mind, it is not always about the total number of visitors, but how interested and ready to buy they are. The further your website visitors are in your sales funnel, the more interested they are in your solution or product, the greater chance you have to increase conversion.

The other big piece of the website traffic equation is your ability to capture the targeted website traffic and convert them into customers, which opens more opportunities for your business to succeed. If you are ready to capture your current website traffic as well as increase your qualified opportunities, then online marketing could be just what your business needs!

7.10 Aside from a website, what else does every business need?

In order to survive and thrive, a business needs a holistic strategy to be both profitable and fulfilling. A holistic model incorporates six areas of business where leaders need minimum competency to be effective leaders and business operators.

7.10.1 Vision

Without a vision that is clear, complete, and compelling, your company will always struggle to reach its full potential. The business may languish in mediocrity, which is almost worse than failure. People perish for lack of vision and so do companies.

7.10.2 Leadership

Strong leadership requires robust health in two parts: your inner game and your outer game. A poor inner game will result in negative, reactive leadership; but a strong inner game will result in stable, strong, creative leadership, the kind of leadership that enables you to empower others.

7.10.3 Management & Operations

You need to understand how to put the right people in the right positions, and then empower them to live into their full potential; this requires that you hire well, train well, and fire well. You also need operating systems in place to efficiently run your business and effectively troubleshoot problems.

7.10.4 Marketing & Sales

Good marketing and sales will turn strangers into raving fans and customers. This includes learning how to use marketing strategies to show customers that your product or service will solve their problem, and make them the hero in their own story.

7.10.5 Money

Business leaders need to learn the basics of money and manage it well, or they risk losing both passion and provision in a single step. Leaders need to have the necessary reports to review and learn how to read them in order to understand the art, analysis, and big picture of how your finances impact your business.

7.10.6 Culture

Everything thrives or dies in relation to its culture. A poor company culture results in disengaged employees who punch a clock just to get their next paycheck. A positive culture results in employees that perform like rock stars for you. Leaders need to develop a healthy culture, both in the physical environment and relationally. A website is an important asset to your business growth strategy. While it fits nicely in the marketing & sales area of business, website traffic will bring you more money that will allow you to boost your management and operations. Most importantly, your website is often the first touch point with a potential customer and your opportunity to answer their questions and make them the hero of their own story.

But it all starts with a company vision, because if you don't have a clear idea of who you are as a company and what you offer, the people who visit your website won't either.

Chapter No. 08

Pros and cons

Social media marketing has become an integral part of the digital landscape, allowing businesses to connect with their target audience, build brand awareness, and drive online traffic. However, like any marketing strategy, it comes with its own set of pros and cons, particularly when it comes to analyzing, monetizing, and managing online traffic. In this discussion, we will explore the various aspects of social media marketing and evaluate its importance in the contemporary business environment.

8.1   Pros of Social Media Marketing

Global Reach and Audience Targeting: Social media platforms provide access to a vast and diverse audience. This global reach allows businesses to target specific demographics based on interests, behavior, location, and other criteria, ensuring that marketing efforts are directed towards the most relevant audience.

Brand Visibility and Awareness: Through consistent and engaging content, businesses can enhance their brand visibility and awareness. Social media platforms serve as virtual billboards where companies can showcase their products or services, share their brand story, and connect with potential customers on a personal level.

Cost-Effective Marketing: Compared to traditional forms of advertising, social media marketing is often more cost-effective. Many platforms offer affordable advertising options, and organic reach can also be significant if the content resonates with the audience.

Real-Time Communication: Social media allows for direct and real-time communication between businesses and their audience. This fosters a sense of community and enables companies to respond promptly to customer inquiries, feedback, and concerns.

Data and Analytics: Social media platforms provide robust analytics tools that allow businesses to track the performance of their marketing efforts. This data includes metrics such as engagement, reach, and conversion rates, helping companies refine their strategies based on measurable results.

Viral Marketing Potential: Engaging and shareable content has the potential to go viral, rapidly reaching a vast audience beyond the initial followers. This can significantly amplify the impact of a marketing campaign and increase brand exposure.

8.2   Cons of Social Media Marketing:

Time-Consuming: Managing social media accounts, creating content, and engaging with the audience can be time-consuming. Businesses need to invest significant effort to maintain an active and effective social media presence.

Algorithm Changes: Social media platforms frequently update their algorithms, affecting the visibility of content. Sudden algorithm changes can impact the reach of organic content and require marketers to adapt their strategies accordingly.

Negative Feedback and Crisis Management: Social media exposes businesses to the risk of negative feedback and public relations crises. A negative comment or viral backlash can harm a brand's reputation, requiring careful management and timely responses.

Saturation and Competition: The popularity of social media has led to a saturated market, making it challenging for businesses to stand out. Competition for attention is fierce, and maintaining visibility requires a strategic approach.

Dependency on Platform Policies: Businesses are subject to the policies and rules of social media platforms. Changes in these policies, such as alterations in content guidelines or advertising rules, can impact marketing strategies and require adjustments.

8.3 Analyzing and Monetizing Social Media

Analytics Tools: Social media platforms offer analytics tools that allow businesses to measure the performance of their content and campaigns. By analyzing metrics such as engagement, impressions, and click-through rates, marketers can gain valuable insights into what works and what needs improvement.

Conversion Tracking: Effective analysis involves tracking conversions, whether they are website visits, product purchases, or other desired actions. This data helps businesses understand the return on investment (ROI) of their social media efforts.

A/B Testing: A/B testing involves creating variations of content and measuring their performance to determine the most effective elements. This experimentation allows businesses to optimize their strategies for better results.

Customer Feedback and Sentiment Analysis: Monitoring customer feedback and sentiment on social media helps businesses understand how their brand is perceived. This information is crucial for making adjustments to marketing strategies and addressing customer concerns.

Monetization Strategies: Social media platforms offer various monetization options, including paid advertising, sponsored content, and influencer partnerships. Businesses can leverage these strategies to generate revenue directly through the platforms.

Affiliate Marketing: Businesses can use social media to engage in affiliate marketing, where they collaborate with influencers or affiliates to promote products or services in exchange for a commission on sales generated through their unique links.

8.3   Importance of Social Media Marketing

Customer Engagement and Loyalty: Social media facilitates direct interaction between businesses and customers, fostering engagement and building brand loyalty. Regular communication and personalized interactions create a sense of community.

Brand Building and Authority: Consistent and positive social media presence contributes to brand building. Through quality content and engagement, businesses can establish themselves as authorities in their industry, gaining trust and credibility.

Traffic Generation and Lead Acquisition: Social media is a powerful tool for driving traffic to a business's website. Well-executed campaigns and compelling content can attract potential customers, generate leads, and ultimately contribute to sales.

Adaptability and Innovation: Social media marketing allows businesses to adapt quickly to market trends and consumer preferences. The dynamic nature of these platforms encourages innovation and experimentation, keeping businesses agile in their marketing strategies.

Competitive Advantage: A robust social media presence can provide a competitive advantage. Businesses that effectively leverage social media are better positioned to reach and engage their target audience, outperform competitors, and adapt to changing market conditions.

In conclusion, while social media marketing offers numerous benefits, it requires careful planning, consistent effort, and adaptability to overcome its challenges. Businesses that invest time and resources in understanding their audience, analyzing data, and refining their strategies are more likely to harness the full potential of social media for marketing purposes. Ultimately, the importance of social media marketing lies in its ability to connect businesses with their audience, drive online traffic, and contribute to long-term success in the digital landscape.

Conclusion

To summarize, "Mastering the Digital Landscape: A Guide to Effective Marketing in the Online Realm" offers a thorough road map that may be used for navigating the ever-changing landscape of social media and digital marketing. The purpose of this book is to provide a strategy roadmap for people and enterprises who are interested in using the power of online platforms to increase traffic, engage audiences, and achieve success in marketing. The central aspect of the book places an emphasis on the significance of control in digital marketing and encourages readers to take responsibility for their presence on the internet. Businesses have the ability to manage their digital narrative, deliberately crafting their brand image and connecting with their target audience, if they take a proactive strategy. The book emphasizes the necessity of keeping up with the ever-changing trends and algorithm changes that occur across the major social media platforms. This helps to ensure that marketing plans continue to be adaptable and successful.

It is one of the most important aspects of the book because it investigates the many internet tools that are essential in increasing the amount of visitors and improving marketing efforts. This book reveals a plethora of resources that are designed to maximize online exposure. These resources range from analytics platforms that shed light on the complexities of audience behavior to search engine optimization tools that improve content for search engines. By making use of these technologies, organizations have the opportunity to get useful insights about their digital performance, improve their strategy, and maintain a competitive advantage over their rivals. A significant amount of focus is placed throughout the book on well-known social media sites as essential routes for achieving success in marketing. Detailed case studies and success stories highlight how companies have used the potential of social media platforms such as Facebook, Instagram, Twitter, and LinkedIn to nurture a client base that is devoted to their brand and to boost brand recognition. Readers are provided with tangible methods to improve their social media game by providing them with practical ideas on how to create interesting content, how to run targeted advertisements, and how to engage with followers.

In addition, the book deals with the mutually beneficial connection that exists between social media and digital marketing respectively. This highlights the need of having a coherent approach that can merge these two areas in a smooth manner, so generating a harmonious presence on the internet. It is possible for companies to establish meaningful relationships with their audience by matching their marketing efforts with the distinctive qualities of each platform. This helps to cultivate trust and loyalty among the audience. In conclusion, the book urges readers to embrace creativity and experimentation in their digital pursuits. This is a farewell remark. As a result of the ever-changing nature of the internet environment, those individuals who are willing to investigate emerging tendencies and technologies will find themselves at the forefront of the digital marketing frontier. It is a compass that guides marketers through the broad and often turbulent terrain of the digital world, eventually allowing them to control their destiny in the vast and ever-expanding digital universe. "Mastering the Digital Landscape" acts as a compass in the enormous threads of the digital domain.